MW00615470
Presents
Common Wildflowers
of Midwestern
North America
The flowers identified in this book can be found in the states of: Illinois,
Indiana, Ohio, Michigan, Iowa, Missouri, Minnesota, Kentucky, and Wisconsin
Pages organized by color making it
easy to find and identify your flower
Each ID Provides:
Flower's common name
Flower's botanical name
Months the flower is found in bloom
Flower Native or Non-native
Year 2021

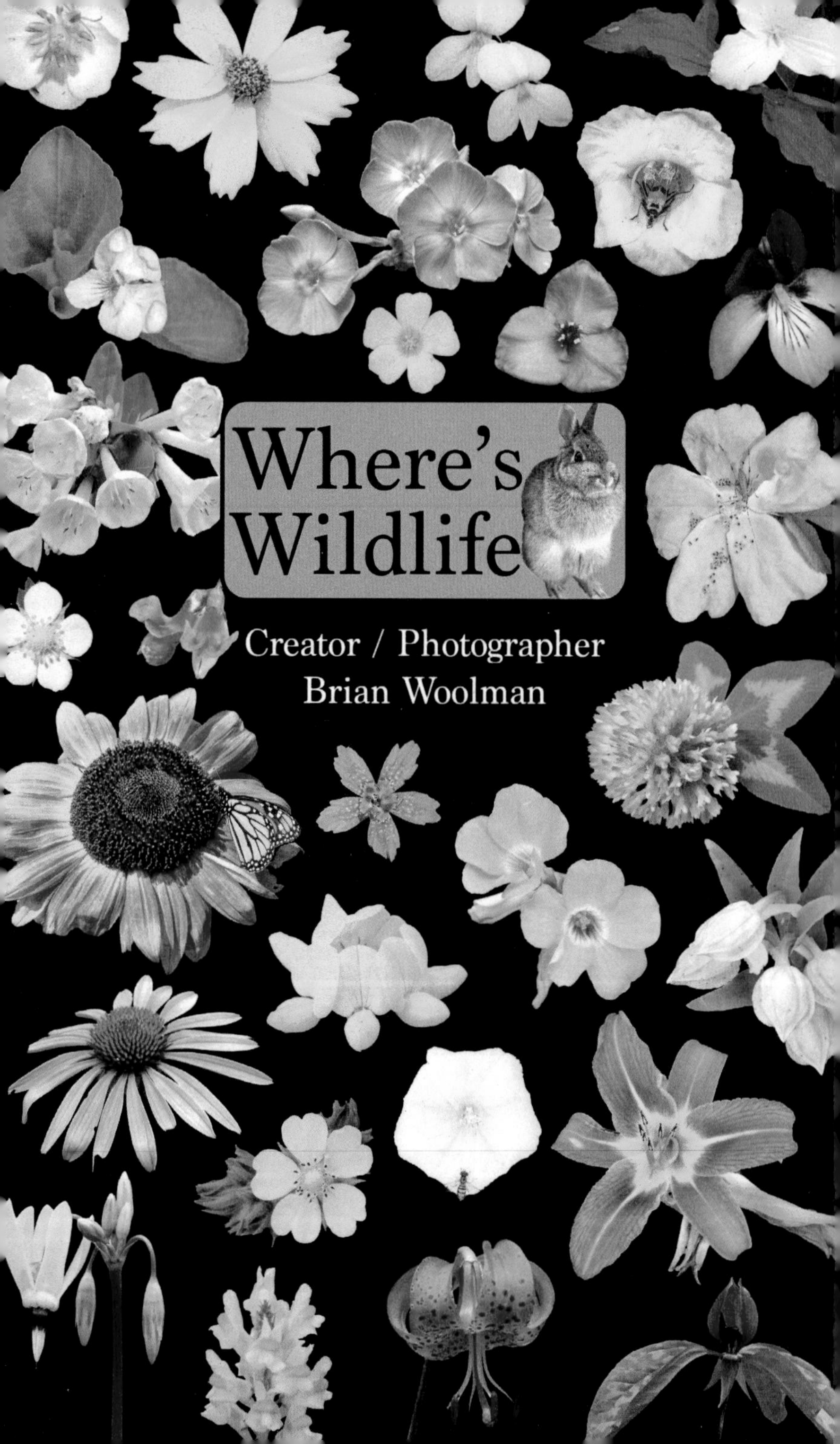
Where's
Wildlife
Creator / Photographer
Brian Woolman

How To Use This Book

The flowers in this book are organized by color for fast and easy identification. Once you determine the dominant color of the flower you want to identify, you flip to that color in this book to quickly narrow down, find, and identify your flower. Each flower identification will include a common name and the botanical name for the species. You will also learn if the flower is a native or non-native species and when the flower can be found in bloom.

Royal Catchfly
(Silene regia)
Native
Found: July - August

Cardinal Flower
(Lobelia cardinalis)
Native
Found: July - September

Fire Pink
(Silene virginica)
Native
Found: April - June

Red Columbine
(Aquilegia canadensis)
Native
Found: May - July

Michigan Lily
(Lilium michiganense)
Native
Found: June - August

Swamp Rose Mallow
(Hibiscus moscheutos)
Native
Found: July - September

Prairie Trillium
(Trillium recurvatum)
Native
Found: April - May

Canadian Wild Ginger
(Asarum canadense)
Native
Found: April - May

Bee Balm
(Monarda didyma)
Native
Found: July - August

Jumpseed
(Persicaria virginiana)
Native
Found: July - September

Curly Dock
(Rumex crispus)
Non-native
Found: June - July

American Lopseed
(Phryma leptostachya)
Native
Found: June - August

Trumpet Creeper
(Campsis radicans)
Native
Found: June - July

Orange Day Lily
(Hemerocallis fulva)
Non-native
Found: July - August

Butterfly Milkweed
(Asclepias tuberosa)
Native
Found: June - August

Orange Jewelweed
(Impatiens capensis)
Native
Found: June - September

Common Sunflower
(Helianthus annuus)
Native
Found: August - October

Common Sunflower
(Helianthus annuus)
Native
Found: August - October

Downy Sunflower
(Helianthus mollis)
Native
Found: July - September

Woodland Sunflower
(Helianthus strumosus)
Native
Found: July - September

Prairie Sunflower
(Helianthus petiolaris)
Native
Found: June - September

Few-leaf Sunflower
(Helianthus occidentalis)
Native
Found: July - September

False Sunflower
(Heliopsis helianthoides)
Native
Found: June - September

Oxeye Sunflower
(Heliopsis helianthoides)
Native
Found: June - August

Black-eyed Susan
(Rudbeckia hirta)
Native
Found: June - October

Orange Coneflower
(Rudbeckia fulgida)
Native
Found: June - October

Brown-eyed Susan
(Rudbeckia triloba)
Native
Found: July - October

Sweet Coneflower
(Rudbeckia subtomentosa)
Native
Found: July - October

Yellow Coneflower
(Ratibida pinnata)
Native
Found: July - September

Tall Coreopsis
(Coreopsis tripteris)
Native
Found: July - September

Bearded Beggarticks
(Bidens aristosa)
Native
Found: August - October

Cut-leaf Coneflower
(Rudbeckia laciniata)
Native
Found: July - September

Lanceleaf Coreopsis
(Coreopsis lanceolata)
Native
Found: May - July

Yellow Goatsbeard
(Tragopogon dubius)
Non-native
Found: June - September

Sneezeweed
(Helenium autumnale)
Native
Found: August - October

Prairie Coreopsis
(Coreopsis palmata)
Native
Found: June - August

Celandine Poppy
(Stylophorum diphyllum)
Native
Found: April - June

Large-flowered False Foxglove
(Aureolaria grandiflora)
Native
Found: June - September

Fringed Loosestrife
(Lysimachia ciliata)
Native
Found: June - August

Fernleaf False Foxglove
(Aureolaria pedicularia)
Native
Found: May - October

Common Evening Primrose
(Oenothera biennis)
Native
Found: July - October

Partridge Pea
(Chamaecrista fasciculata)
Native
Found: June - October

Common Mullein
(Verbascum thapsus)
Non-native
Found: June - September

Tall Thimbleweed
(Anemone virginiana)
Native
Found: June - August

Swamp Buttercup
(Ranunculus septentrionalis)
Native
Found: April - June

Creeping Jenny
(Lysimachia nummularia)
Non-native
Found: June - August

Tall Buttercup
(Ranunculus acris)
Non-native
Found: May - October

Marsh Marigold
(Caltha palustris)
Native
Found: April - June

Common Cinquefoil
(Potentilla simplex)
Native
Found: May - July

Shrubby Cinquefoil
(Dasiphora fruticosa)
Native
Found: July - September

Sulfur Cinquefoil
(Potentilla recta)
Non-native
Found: June - August

Brook Cinquefoil
(Potentilla rivalis)
Native
Found: June - Augsut

Seedbox
(Ludwigia alternifolia)
Native
Found: June - August

Yellow Star-grass
(Hypoxis hirsuta)
Native
Found: May - July

Yellow Jewelweed
(Impatiens pallida)
Native
Found: July - September

Yellow Avens
(Geum aleppicum)
Native
Found: June - July

Meadow Hawkweed
(Hieracium caespitosum)
Non-native
Found: June - August

Field Hawkweed
(Pilosella caespitosa)
Non-native
Found: June - August

Two-flowered Cynthia
(Krigia biflora)
Native
Found: May - August

Perennial Sowthistle
(Sonchus arvensis)
Non-native
Found: July - October

Dandelion
(Taraxacum officinale)
Non-native
Found: March - November

Little-leaf Buttercup
(Ranunculus abortivus)
Native
Found: April - June

Carolina Puccoon
(Lithospermum caroliniense)
Native
Found: May - July

Cursed Crowfoot
(Ranunculus sceleratus)
Native
Found: May - September

Spotted St. John's-wort
(Hypericum punctatum)
Native
Found: June - August

Dwarf St. John's Wort
(Hypericum mutilum)
Native
Found: June - August

Shrubby St. John's-wort
(Hypericum prolificum)
Native
Found: June - August

Low Hop Clover
(Trifolium campestre)
Non-native
Found: May - September

Prairie Dock
(Silphium terebinthinaceum)
Native
Found: August - October

Compass Plant
(Silphium laciniatum)
Native
Found: July - September

Rosinweed
(Silphium integrifolium)
Native
Found: July - September

Giant Sunflower
(Helianthus giganteus)
Native
Found: July - September

Birdsfoot Trefoil
(Lotus corniculatus)
Non-native
Found: June - August

Prickly Lettuce
(Lactuca serriola)
Non-native
Found: July - September

American Gromwell
(Lithospermum latifolium)
Native
Found: May - June

Southern Wood Sorrel
(Oxalis dillenii)
Native
Found: May - October

Trumpet Daffodil
(Narcissus pseudonarcissus)
Non-native
Found: January - April

Flower-of-an-Hour
(Hibiscus trionum)
Non-native
Found: June - October

Yellow Iris
(Iris pseudacorus)
Non-native
Found: May - July

Hairy Yellow Violet
(Viola pubescens pubescens)
Native
Found: April - June

Field Mustard
(Brassica rapa)
Non-native
Found: May - July

Wild Mustard
(Sinapis arvensis)
Non-native
Found: May - July

Yellow Rocket
(Barbarea vulgaris)
Non-native
Found: April - June

Tall Tumble Mustard
(Sisymbrium altissimum)
Non-native
Found: June - August

Butterweed
(Packera glabella)
Native
Found: April - June

Clammy Ground Cherry
(Physalis heterophylla)
Native
Found: June - September

Field Milkwort
(Polygala sanguinea)
Native
Found: July - September

Virginia Ground Cherry
(Physalis virginiana)
Native
Found: June - August

Tufted Loosestrife
(Lysimachia thyrsiflora)
Native
Found: May - July

Wild Parsnip
(Pastinaca sativa)
Non-native
Found: June - July

Wild Black Currant
(Ribes americanum)
Native
Found: May - June

False Solomon's Seal
(Maianthemum racemosum)
Native
Found: May - June

Swamp Agrimony
(Agrimonia parviflora)
Native
Found: July - September

Canada Milkvetch
(Astragalus canadensis)
Native
Found: June - August

Tall Hairy Agrimony
(Agrimonia gryposepala)
Native
Found: June - September

Yellow Sweet Clover
(Melilotus officinalis)
Non-native
Found: June - September

Spatterdock
(Nuphar advena)
Native
Found: June - August

Nodding Bur-Marigold
(Bidens cernua)
Native
Found: July - October

Creeping Water Primrose
(Ludwigia peploides)
Native
Found: June - September

Yellow Bellwort
(Uvularia grandiflora)
Native
Found: April - June

Scouring Rush
(Eutrochium maculatum)
Native
Found: June - September

Round-headed Bush Clover
(Lespedeza capitata)
Native
Found: July - September

Wild Four O'Clock
(Mirabilis nyctaginea)
Native
Found: May - September

Butter and Eggs
(Linaria vulgaris)
Non-native
Found: June - October

Early Goldenrod
(Solidago juncea)
Native
Found: July - September

Giant Goldenrod
(Solidago gigantea)
Native
Found: August - October

Canada Goldenrod
(Solidago canadensis)
Native
Found: July - October

Stiff Goldenrod
(Solidago rigida)
Native
Found: August - September

Zigzag Goldenrod
(Solidago flexicaulis)
Native
Found: August - October

Grass-leaved Goldenrod
(Euthamia graminifolia)
Native
Found: July - September

Elm-leaved Goldenrod
(Solidago ulmifolia)
Native
Found: July - September

Wild Geranium
(Geranium maculatum)
Native
Found: April - June

Common Blue Violet
(Viola sororia)
Native
Found: March - May

Labrador Violet
(Viola labradorica)
Native
Found: April - May

Common Chicory
(Cichorium intybus)
Non-native
Found: July - October

Birdsfoot Violet
(Viola pedata)
Native
Found: April - June

Lesser Periwinkle
(Vinca minor)
Non-native
Found: April - June

Jacob's Ladder
(Polemonium reptans)
Native
Found: April - June

Hairy Wild Petunia
(Ruellia humilis)
Native
Found: May - October

Kalm's Lobelia
(Lobelia kalmii)
Native
Found: July - September

Ground Ivy
(Glechoma hederacea)
Non-native
Found: March - July

Ohio Spiderwort
(Tradescantia ohiensis)
Native
Found: May - July

Allegheny Monkey Flower
(Mimulus ringens)
Native
Found: June - September

Asiatic Dayflower
(Commelina communis)
Non-native
Found: July - August

Blue-eyed Grass
(Sisyrinchium angustifolium)
Native
Found: May - June

Cornflower
(Centaurea cyanus)
Non-native
Found: May - July

American Bellflower
(Campanula americana)
Native
Found: July - October

Field Milkwort
(Polygala sanguinea)
Native
Found: July - September

Creeping Bellflower
(Campanula rapunculoides)
Non-native
Found: June - October

Blue False Indigo
(Baptisia australis)
Native
Found: May - June

Dwarf Larkspur
(Delphinium tricorne)
Native
Found: April - May

Pokeweed
(Phytolacca americana)
Native
Found: July - September

Great Blue Lobelia
(Lobelia siphilitica)
Native
Found: July - October

Fringed Gentian
(Gentianopsis crinita)
Native
Found: August - November

Bottle Gentian
(Gentiana andrewsii)
Native
Found: August - September

Self-Heal
(Prunella vulgaris)
Native
Found: June - October

Marsh Blazingstar
(Liatris spicata)
Native
Found: July - August

Sage
(Geranium maculatum)
Non-native
Found: June - September

Rough Blazingstar
(Liatris aspera)
Native
Found: August - September

Prairie Blazing Star
(Liatris pycnostachya)
Native
Found: July - August

Hoary Verbena
(Verbena stricta)
Native
Found: July - September

Blue Vervain
(Verbena hastata)
Native
Found: June - October

Pickerelweed
(Pontederia cordata)
Native
Found: June - September

Leadplant
(Amorpha canescens)
Native
Found: June - August

Round-lobed Hepatica
(Hepatica americana)
Native
Found: April - May

Virginia Bluebells
(Mertensia virginica)
Native
Found: March - May

Siberian Squill
(Scilla sibirica)
Non-native
Found: April

Bittersweet Nightshade
(Solanum dulcamara)
Non-native
Found: June - September

American Vetch
(Vicia americana)
Native
Found: May - September

Broadleaf Wild Leek
(Allium ampeloprasum)
Non-Native
Found: Seasonal

Hairy Vetch
(Vicia villosa)
Non-native
Found: June - August

Alfalfa
(Medicago sativa)
Non-native
Found: June - September

Siberian Bugloss
(Brunnera macrophylla)
Non-native
Found: April - May

Wild Bergamot
(Monarda fistulosa)
Native
Found: July - September

True Forget-me-not
(Myosotis scorpioides)
Non-native
Found: May - August

Virginia Iris
(Iris virginica)
Native
Found: May - July

Fogfruit
(Phyla lanceolata)
Native
Found: June - September

Blue Wood Aster
(Symphyotrichum cordifolium)
Native
Found: August - October

New England Aster
(Symphyotrichum novae-angliae)
Native
Found: August - October

Smooth Blue Aster
(Symphyotrichum laeve)
Native
Found: August - October

American Sea-rocket
(Cakile edentula)
Native
Found: July - September

Missouri Ironweed
(Vernonia missurica)
Native
Found: July - August

Downy Wood Mint
(Blephilia ciliata)
Native
Found: May - August

Tall Ironweed
(Vernonia gigantea)
Native
Found: July - September

Hog Peanut
(Amphicarpaea bracteata)
Native
Found: July - September

Winged Loosestrife
(Lythrum alatum)
Native
Found: June - September

Mad-dog Skullcap
(Scutellaria lateriflora)
Native
Found: July - October

Wild Lupine
(Lupinus perennis)
Native
Found: May - August

Woodland Phlox
(Phlox divaricata)
Native
Found: April- June

Virginia Spring Beauty
(Claytonia virginica)
Native
Found: April - June

Woodland Crocus
(Crocus tommasinianus)
Non-native
Found: March

Prairie Rose
(Rosa arkansana)
Native
Found: June – July

Swamp Rose Mallow
(Hibiscus moscheutos)
Native
Found: July - September

Wild Geranium
(Geranium maculatum)
Native
Found: April - June

Halberd-Leaved Rose Mallow
(Hibiscus laevis)
Native
Found: August - September

Hedge Bindweed
(Calystegia sepium)
Native
Found: June - September

Violet Wood-sorrel
(Oxalis violacea)
Native
Found: April - June

Slender False Foxglove
(Agalinis tenuifolia)
Native
Found: August - October

Marsh Pea
(Lathyrus palustris)
Native
Found: June - July

Purple False Foxglove
(Agalinis purpurea)
Native
Found: August - October

Deptford Pink
(Dianthus armeria)
Non-native
Found: June - September

Rue Anemone
(Thalictrum thalictroides)
Native
Found: March - June

Branching Centaury
(Centaurium pulchellum)
Non-native
Found: June – October

Rosepink
(Sabatia angularis)
Native
Found: July - August

Summer Phlox
(Phlox paniculata)
Native
Found: July - September

Virginia Bluebells
(Mertensia virginica)
Native
Found: April - May

Dame's Rocket
(Hesperis matronalis)
Non-native
Found: May - July

Wild Bergamot
(Monarda fistulosa)
Native
Found: July - September

Swamp Thistle
(Cirsium muticum)
Native
Found: July - October

Field Thistle
(Nabalus albus)
Native
Found: June - September

Musk Thistle
(Carduus nutans)
Non-native
Found: June - October

Spotted Knapweed
(Centaurea biebersteinii)
Non-native
Found: June - October

Bull Thistle
(Cirsium vulgare)
Non-native
Found: June - October

Field Milkwort
(Polygala sanguinea)
Native
Found: July - September

Canada Thistle
(Cirsium arvense)
Non-native
Found: June - October

Red Clover
(Trifolium pratense)
Non-native
Found: June - September

Obedient Plant
(Physostegia virginiana)
Native
Found: June - September

American Germander
(Teucrium canadense)
Native
Found: July - August

Marsh Hedge Nettle
(Stachys palustris)
Native
Found: June - August

Purple Rattlesnake-root
(Prenanthes racemosa)
Native
Found: August - October

Prairie Blazing Star
(Liatris pycnostachya)
Native
Found: July - September

Purple Prairie Clover
(Dalea purpurea)
Native
Found: June - August

Purple Loosestrife
(Lythrum salicaria)
Non-native
Found: July - September

Showy Tick-trefoil
(Desmodium canadense)
Native
Found: July - September

Illinois Tick-trefoil
(Desmodium illinoense)
Native
Found: July - August

Motherwort
(Leonurus cardiaca)
Non-native
Found: June - August

Hoary Verbena
(Verbena stricta)
Native
Found: July - September

Pokeweed
(Phytolacca americana)
Native
Found: July - September

Pennsylvania Smartweed
(Persicaria pensylvanica)
Native
Found: June - September

Creeping Smartweed
(Persicaria longiseta)
Non-native
Found: July - October

Lady's Thumb
(Persicaria maculosa)
Non-native
Found: June - September

Waterpepper
(Persicaria hydropiper)
Non-native
Found: July - September

Swamp Smartweed
(Persicaria hydropiperoides)
Native
Found: June - September

Purple Coneflower
(Echinacea purpurea)
Native
Found: June - October

Water Smartweed
(Persicaria amphibia)
Native
Found: June - September

Nodding Onion
(Allium cernuum)
Native
Found: June - August

Pointed-leaf Tick-trefoil
(Desmodium glutinosum)
Native
Found: June - August

Shooting Star
(Dodecatheon meadia)
Native
Found: April - June

Limestone Bittercress
(Cardamine douglassii)
Native
Found: March - May

Purple-leaf Willowherb
(Epilobium coloratum)
Native
Found: July - October

Common Milkweed
(Asclepias syriaca)
Native
Found: June - August

Crown Vetch
(Securigera varia)
Non-native
Found: May - September

Cornflower
(Centaurea cyanus)
Non-native
Found: May - July

Alsike Clover
(Trifolium hybridum)
Non-native
Found: June - September

Joe-Pye Weed
(Eutrochium fistulosum)
Native
Found: July - September

Showy Lady's-slipper
(Cypripedium reginae)
Native
Found: June - July

Spotted Joe-Pye Weed
(Eutrochium maculatum)
Native
Found: July - September

Showy Orchid
(Galearis spectabilis)
Native
Found: April - May

White Lettuce
(Nabalus albus)
Native
Found: July - September

Wild Four O'Clock
(Mirabilis nyctaginea)
Native
Found: May - September

Swamp Milkweed
(Asclepias incarnata)
Native
Found: July - August

Soapwort
(Saponaria officinali)
Non-native
Found: June - September

Prairie Crabapple
(Malus ioensis)
Native
Found: May - June

Groundnut
(Apios americana)
Native
Found: July - September

Missouri Gooseberry
(Ribes missouriense)
Native
Found: April - June

Eastern Redbud
(Cercis canadensis)
Native
Found: April - May

Ditch Stonecrop
(Penthorum sedoides)
Native
Found: July - September

Bloodroot
(Sanguinaria canadensis)
Native
Found: March - April

Early Meadow Rue
(Thalictrum dioicum)
Native
Found: April - June

Bluntleaf Sandwort
(Moehringia lateriflora)
Native
Found: May - June

White Trillium
(Trillium grandiflorum)
Native
Found: April - June

Drooping Trillium
(Trillium flexipes)
Native
Found: May - June

Sawtooth Blackberry
(Calystegia sepium)
Native
Found: April - June

May-apple
(Podophyllum peltatum)
Native
Found: April - May

Rue Anemone
(Thalictrum thalictroides)
Native
Found: March - June

Canada Anemone
(Anemonastrum canadense)
Native
Found: April - June

False Rue-anemone
(Enemion biternatum)
Native
Found: March - May

Wood Anemone
(Anemone quinquefolia)
Native
Found: April - June

Tall Meadow Rue
(Thalictrum dasycarpum)
Native
Found: June - July

Garden Valerian
(Valeriana officinalis)
Non-native
Found: June - October

Black Cherry
(Prunus serotina)
Native
Found: April - May

Blackhaw
(Viburnum prunifolium)
Native
Found: May - June

Common Chickweed
(Stellaria media)
Non-native
Found: June - September

White Avens
(Geum canadense)
Native
Found: May - July

Mouse-ear Chickweed
(Cerastium fontanum)
Non-native
Found: May - September

Tall Thimbleweed
(Anemone virginiana)
Native
Found: June - August

Wild Strawberry
(Fragaria virginiana)
Native
Found: April - May

Tall Cinquefoil
(Drymocallis arguta)
Native
Found: June - August

Broadleaf Arrowhead
(Sagittaria latifolia)
Native
Found: July - September

Multiflora Rose
(Rosa multiflora)
Non-native
Found: June - July

Foxglove Beardtongue
(Penstemon digitalis)
Native
Found: May - June

Moth Mullein
(Verbascum blattaria)
Non-native
Found: June - September

Pale-Spiked Lobelia
(Lobelia spicata)
Native
Found: June - August

Soapwort
(Saponaria officinalis)
Non-native
Found: June - September

Rose of Sharon
(Hibiscus syriacus)
Non-native
Found: June - October

Field Bindweed
(Convolvulus arvensis)
Non-native
Found: June - September

Swamp Rose Mallow
(Hibiscus moscheutos)
Native
Found: July - September

Hedge Bindweed
(Calystegia sepium)
Non-native
Found: June - September

Ox-eye Daisy
(Leucanthemum vulgare)
Non-native
Found: May - August

Striped Cream Violet
(Viola striata)
Native
Found: April - June

Poet's Daffodil
(Narcissus poeticus)
Non-native
Found: February - April

Carolina Horsenettle
(Solanum carolinense)
Native
Found: May - September
139

White Trout Lily
(Erythronium albidum)
Native
Found: April - May

White Campion
(Silene latifolia)
Non-native
Found: May - September

Starry Campion
(Silene stellata)
Native
Found: June - August

Bladder Campion
(Silene vulgaris)
Non-native
Found: June - October

Wild Bergamot
(Monarda fistulosa)
Native
Found: July - September

Common Mountain Mint
(Pycnanthemum virginianum)
Native
Found: July - September

Wild Quinine
(Parthenium integrifolium)
Native
Found: June - September

Guelder-rose
(Viburnum opulus)
Non-native
Found: April - May

New Jersey Tea
(Ceanothus americanus)
Native
Found: May - June

Hoary Alyssum
(Berteroa incana)
Non-native
Found: April - October

Field Pennycress
(Thlaspi arvense)
Non-native
Found: April - June

White Meadowsweet
(Spiraea alba)
Native
Found: June - September

Wild Hyacinth
(Camassia scilloides)
Native
Found: April - May

White Clover
(Trifolium campestre)
Non-native
Found: May - October

White Sweet Clover
(Melilotus alba)
Non-native
Found: June - October

White Prairie Clover
(Dalea candida)
Native
Found: May - July

Star of Bethlehem
(*Ornithogalum umbellatum*)
Non-native
Found: May - June

Flowering Spurge
(*Euphorbia corollata*)
Native
Found: June - September

White Goldenrod
(Solidago ptarmicoides)
Native
Found: July - September

Flat-topped White Aster
(Doellingeria umbellata)
Native
Found: July - October

Sweet Everlasting
(Pseudognaphalium obtusifolium)
Native
Found: July - October

Tall Boneset
(Eupatorium altissimum)
Native
Found: August - September

Whorled Milkweed
(Asclepias verticillata)
Native
Found: June - September

White Snakeroot
(Ageratina altissima)
Native
Found: July - August

Culver's Root
(Veronicastrum virginicum)
Native
Found: June - August

White False Indigo
(Baptisia alba)
Native
Found: May - June

Yellow Giant Hyssop
(Agastache nepetoides)
Native
Found: July - October

Catnip
(Nepeta cataria)
Non-native
Found: May - September

Pokeweed
(Phytolacca americana)
Native
Found: July - September

Pale Smartweed
(Persicaria lapathifolia)
Native
Found: July - September

Erect Hedge Parsley
(Torilis japonica)
Non-native
Found: June - August

Common Peppergrass
(Lepidium virginicum)
Native
Found: May - September

Prairie Fleabane
(Erigeron strigosus)
Native
Found: June - September

Snowdrop
(Galanthus nivalis)
Non-native
Found: February - March

Philadelphia Fleabane
(Erigeron philadelphicus)
Native
Found: May - June

Nodding Onion
(Allium cernuum)
Native
Found: June - August

White Turtlehead
(Chelone glabra)
Native
Found: August - September

Dutchman's Breeches
(Dicentra cucullaria)
Native
Found: March - April

Cream Gentian
(*Gentiana flavida*)
Native
Found: August - October

American White Waterlily
(*Nymphaea odorata*)
Native
Found: March - October

Jumpseed
(Persicaria virginiana)
Native
Found: July - September

Prairie Indian Plantain
(Arnoglossum plantagineum)
Native
Found: June - August

Nodding Ladies'-tresses
(Spiranthes cernua)
Native
Found: July - September

Pale Indian Plantain
(Arnoglossum atriplicifolium)
Native
Found: July - August

Buttonbush
(Cephalanthus occidentalis)
Non-native
Found: June - September

Dandelion
(Taraxacum officinale)
Non-native
Found: March - November

Cut-Leaved Teasel
(Dipsacus laciniatus)
Non-native
Found: July - September

Yellow Goatsbeard
(Tragopogon dubius)
Non-native
Found: June - September

Wild Mint
(Mentha arvensis)
Native
Found: July - September

Wild Leek
(Allium tricoccum)
Native
Found: June - July

Virginia Waterleaf
(Hydrophyllum virginianum)
Native
Found: May - June

Tall Meadow Rue
(Thalictrum dasycarpum)
Native
Found: June - July

Spring Cress
(Cardamine bulbosa)
Native
Found: April - June

Enchanter's Nightshade
(Circaea lutetiana)
Native
Found: June - August

Sand Croton
(Croton glandulosus)
Native
Found: July - October

Cleavers
(Galium aparine)
Native
Found: May - June

Biennial Gaura
(Gaura biennis)
Native
Found: June - August

Common Yarrow
(Achillea millefolium)
Native
Found: June - September

Crown Vetch
(Securigera varia)
Non-native
Found: May - September

Rattlesnake Master
(Eryngium yuccifolium)
Native
Found: June - September

Amur Honeysuckle
(Lonicera maackii)
Non-native
Found: May - June

Queen Anne's Lace
(Daucus carota)
Non-native
Found: June - September

Garlic Mustard
(Alliaria petiolata)
Non-native
Found: May - June

Wild Plum
(Prunus americana)
Native
Found: May - June

Wild Calla
(Calla palustris)
Native
Found: May - June

Shooting Star
(Dodecatheon meadia)
Native
Found: April - May

Swamp Lousewort
(Pedicularis lanceolata)
Native
Found: August - September

Spotted Bee Balm
(Monarda punctata)
Native
Found: July - September

INDEX

INDEX

INDEX

INDEX

INDEX

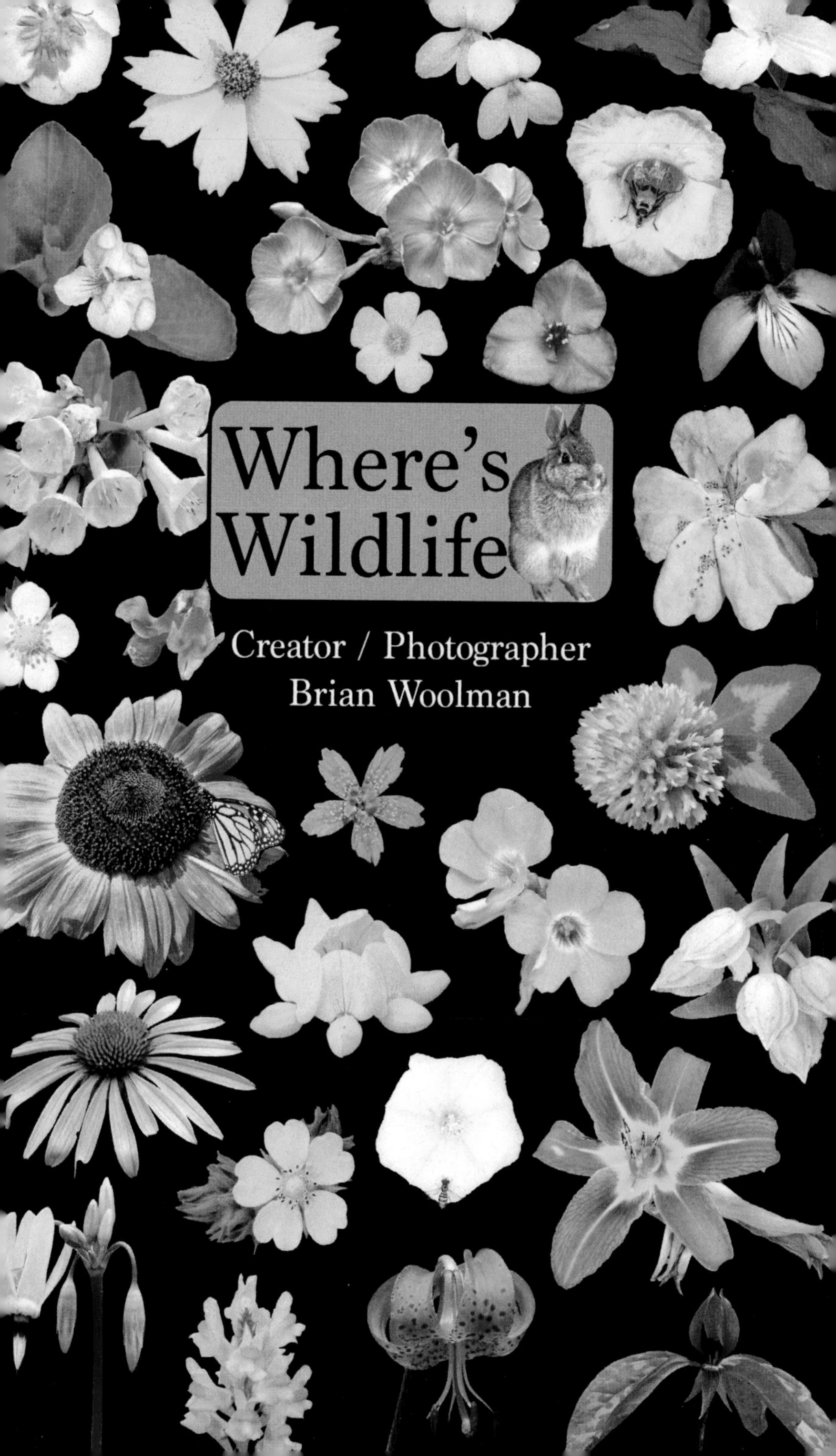
Where's
Wildlife
Creator / Photographer
Brian Woolman

Where's Wildlife
Presents
Common Wildflowers of Midwestern North America
The flowers identified in this book can be found in the states of: Illinois, Indiana, Ohio, Michigan, Iowa, Missouri, Minnesota, Kentucky, and Wisconsin
Pages organized by color making it easy to find and identify your flower
Each ID Provides:
Flower's common name
Flower's botanical name
Months the flower is found in bloom
Flower Native or Non-native
Year 2021